Where Do Old Stuffed Animals Go?

(When They Die)

Written and Illustrated by

Sandra L. Lambert

PAGE PUBLISHING
Conneaut Lake, PA

First originally published by Page Publishing 2024

ISBN 979-8-89315-439-9 (pbk)
ISBN 979-8-89315-455-9 (digital)

Printed in the United States of America

To my nephews Paxton, Sawyer, Sylas, and niece Saylor, I hope you always dream big. Never be afraid to let your imaginations soar to new heights! Remember that you are loved by me. Most of all, you are loved by your Creator!

Always with love,

Aunt Sandra

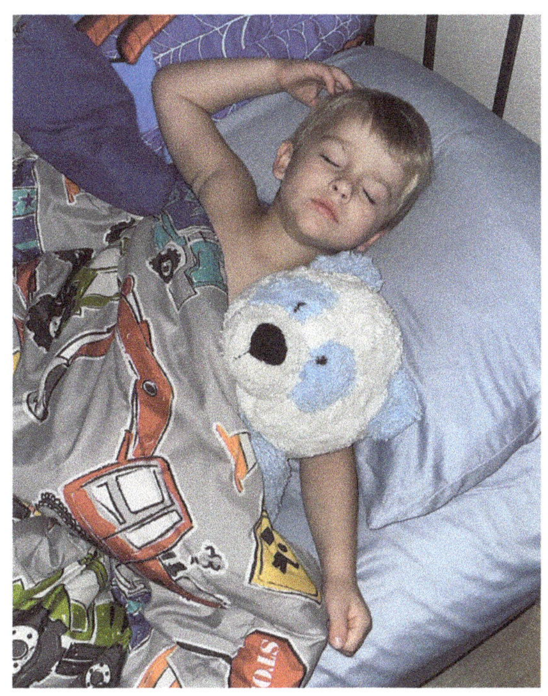

When babies are born, they are usually given gifts from family and friends. New babies mostly get things like clothes, diapers, or bottles and other supplies. But sometimes, toys are given, toys such as stuffed animals! Stuffed animals also make good gifts for birthdays and Christmas.

Some children may be given a stuffed animal that resembles a little brown horse, a fuzzy pink bunny, or even a gray elephant with funny big ears! To a child, these animals become more than just a toy; they become friends. Friends who are cared for and loved for many years to come!

Welcome Baby
A gift for Baby

When baby Sawyer was born, he received a teddy bear, just as his

big brother Pax and sister Saylor (who was only a little older) once did.

Saylor had gotten her favorite stuffed bear as a birthday gift. She and

Sawyer both became attached to their bears!

Different from most stuffed bears, which are normally brown and tan, Sawyer's bear was a bit unusual. The bear, whom he lovingly called "Buddy," was white, with blue arms, legs, and ears. Buddy even had patches of blue fur around his eyes. However, Sawyer believed Buddy was perfect for him!

As time went by, baby Sawyer grew into a young boy. Sawyer and his bear Buddy had many fun adventures. They would watch their favorite shows on television. They shared their favorite snacks together. Sawyer would take Buddy outdoors to play on the swing set. Sometimes big sister Saylor would join them. Saylor liked pushing Sawyer on the swing!

One day, after the recent death of Grandpa, who had been sick in the hospital and was very old, Sawyer began to think. He asked himself, "I wonder where old stuffed animals go when they die?" Little Sawyer had become very attached to his stuffed bear, as he had been to Grandpa. He did not want to lose him too. He did not want Buddy to go away like Grandpa did.

13

Sometime later, Sawyer went shopping with his mom to a resale store. He saw all kinds of used items for sale. There were shoes, shirts, pants, and coats. There were also pots, pans, lamps, and mirrors. And of course, there were toys! Sawyer looked at all the shelves of toys. It was all very exciting! But one shelf caught his eye more than the rest. It was a shelf full of stuffed animals! Sawyer asked his mom in a soft voice, "Is this where old stuffed animals go when they die?"

His mom, looking puzzled, whispered back, "No, this is where they go when children stop playing with them, so they can be resold to children who will play with them."

Feeling his question had not been answered, Sawyer was still confused. So he decided to ask his brother and sister. "Where do old stuffed animals go when they die?" the boy mumbled.

Pax just kept playing his game as if he never heard the question. Saylor shrugged her shoulders and replied, "I don't know. Don't ask me!"

Days later, when he went back to school, Sawyer asked the same question to a few of his friends and classmates, but no one had an answer. Not even the teacher!

School

GOD LOVES ME

The years soon passed, Sawyer and Buddy the bear had many more adventures. They would play hide-and-seek, build forts, and climb trees together. Sometimes they would ride toy tractors or read books. At night, when Sawyer grew tired from a long day of play, he and Buddy would sleep together. And Sawyer would dream!

As even more time passed by, Sawyer grew older. He spent less time playing with Buddy and became interested in new things. Being tattered and worn from years of play, the bear was placed on a shelf in the closet! The boy's mom didn't have the heart to give it away. Each time she opened the closet door to hang clothes, she would see Buddy's face staring back at her. Though Sawyer had forgotten, she remembered the question he asked her years ago: "Is this where old stuffed animals go when they die?" Feeling a bit sad as she closed the closet door, a thought suddenly came to her as she rubbed her tummy.

No, stuffed animals do not die, they live forever in the memories, hearts, and dreams of the children who have loved them!

The End

Sandra was born and raised in the rural South. As a child, she grew up with her siblings in an abundance of nature. In her younger days, Sandra developed a very vivid imagination. She began writing short stories at an early age. Often, she would create art to depict her stories. Art and writing were always a huge part of Sandra's life growing up. She would create artwork for various school projects, such as book reports and essays. Later, Sandra continued writing short stories and began writing poems also. Occasionally, she would win awards for her writings. Down through the years, her love for imagination and storytelling grew. Sandra soon gravitated toward writing her own style of children's books. Sandra hopes to continue using her creativity and imagination, along with her own artwork, to entertain children for years to come.